HEARTBREAK

Other titles in this
series include:

HEARTBREAK

Published in 2019 by The School of Life
First published in the USA in 2020
70 Marchmont Street, London WC1N 1AB
Copyright © The School of Life 2019
Printed in Belgium by Graphius

A proportion of this book has appeared online at
www.theschooloflife.com/thebookoflife

Every effort has been made to contact the copyright holders of
the material reproduced in this book. If any have been inadvertently
overlooked, the publisher will be pleased to make restitution at the
earliest opportunity.

The School of Life is a resource for helping us understand ourselves, for
improving our relationships, our careers and our social lives – as well as
for helping us find calm and get more out of our leisure hours. We do
this through creating films, workshops, books and gifts.
www.theschooloflife.com

ISBN 978-1-912891-01-6

10 9 8 7 6 5 4 3 2

Cover image: Diogo Sousa / p.63 Black Country Images, Alamy

CONTENTS

INTRODUCTION

They used to love us. We used to have a future. We would fall asleep in their arms.

We shared our fears and gave them a map to our insecurities. We loved their sense of humour and perspective on our lives. We travelled with them, understood their feelings for their parents, perhaps even decorated a home together. They were our best friend.

And now we are devastated.

We dignify this special pain with a powerful name: *heartbreak* – because it simply feels as if something essential, something fundamental, in us has shattered. We struggle to describe quite what we are going through. Sometimes, for a few hours, it seems we will almost cope. Then we are abruptly reminded that everything good has gone from the world. What we feel most of all is alone – alone with the sadness and confusion, the anger and the incomprehension.

One of the biggest ambitions of art has been to meet us in the dark, to join us when we're broken and lost – and to remind us of things which, at this moment, we find hard to see: that our pain makes sense, that we are still viable, loveable people, that we will recover and that, however individual the precise details of our suffering may be, we are in fact participating in a sorrow that is common to many.

Everyone we admire, everyone we find interesting has had, or will have, their heart broken. Our heartbreak seems to cut us off from the rest of humanity – secretly it brings us closer together.

What follows is a journey around the universal story of heartbreak.

WHY DID THEY LEAVE US?

They've gone – and what we need most of all is to understand *why*?

What is striking is that, despite what friends and well-meaning acquaintances tell us, we already know. It is us.

We firmly and naturally assume that the explanation has to do with our miserable failings, our dispiriting character and our wearisome appearance. They've gone because we weren't good enough. They got to know us intimately, far better than almost anyone else has ever done and then, inevitably, they saw the truth behind our characters and were horrified. It is not the relationship that failed: We failed.

But, counter-intuitively, what seems most obvious to us in our hearts might not actually be true. There is a famous experiment in the history of psychology which pinpoints our tendency to project: that is, to read decisive, clear explanations drawn from our minds into what are in fact ambiguous situations in the world beyond us.

The Thematic Apperception Test (TAT), as it is technically known, was developed in the 1930s by the American psychologist Henry Murray. It presents us with a series of images and asks us to say what is going on. People tend have quite specific ideas of what is

The Thematic Apperception Test consisted of images, similar to this one, showing provocative, ambiguous scenes.

happening in each scenario. For example, based on the picture above a number of conclusions could be drawn:

- She is fed up with him; he is weak and a bit boring.
- She has just told him that their relationship isn't working and that she is leaving.
- He has just told her they have to break up and the reason has something to do with their sex life. He is not as fulfilled as he wants to be.

- It seems to be about his parents. She wants him to distance himself from them. If he doesn't, she can't be expected to stay around forever.

The power of the experiment derives from the fact that the image has, by design, no definite significance: They're just actors carefully asked to assume certain ambiguous poses. The stories and the meanings come from us.

This is often exactly what happens around our own heartbreaks. We may never actually know precisely why the other person left us. However well we know someone, they are never fully transparent to us. What they say may be only a part of what is really on their mind. Their deeper motives remain obscure – perhaps even to them. We're presented with a fact – they have left us – and on to that we project a meaning. But the meaning we give to the fact comes, in large part, from us.

Admitting to ourselves that we won't always understand another person's inner workings is an underused and powerful skill. At one of the foundational moments of philosophy in ancient Athens, Socrates argued that a huge component of wisdom lies in our capacity to accept our ignorance in certain situations: 'The wise know when they don't know'. This recognition of not-knowing, and the reminder of our tendency to project, may be helpful in easing us away from the more catastrophic and self-incriminating interpretations of a break-up.

The lover who furiously told us they never wanted to see us again may, in the hidden recesses of their soul, have actually been thinking: 'I'm so sad this didn't work out; I wish I could find a way to make this work; you are so lovely in many ways, but there's something desperate in me that's turning away from your offer of love.' The person who coldly texts us, 'That's it, I'm out' may, behind the scenes, be weeping at their own sense of loss and failure rather than (as we imagine) gleefully celebrating the end of their over-extended encounter with us. The person who says, 'I wish this could work, but I've got to concentrate on my career' might actually be sincere rather than (as we might darkly suppose) putting a polite cover over their contempt for us.

The acceptance of ambiguity is liberating: We're free to recognise that the ending wasn't necessarily all our fault; that there may have been forces at work other than our own inadequacy. We're still very sad, but the target of our misery is a little more bearable: We can focus on the deep, sorrowful strangeness of love and loss rather than suffering an extended excoriating confrontation with our own inadequacies.

UNFAIR DISMISSAL IN LOVE

Our lover has wounded us deeply. Our suffering is comparable to being robbed or physically assaulted. In a way, this hurts more than someone stealing our phone or bicycle. However, in those cases, there are big societal mechanisms for addressing our suffering: There are insurance companies, police forces, courts and ultimately prisons designed to restore justice. If an employer suddenly decides that they can't stand us, they usually can't indiscriminately drop us: All kinds of rights and safeguards have been slowly and wisely established to protect our employment from whims and cruelty. Culturally, we've focused our collective systems of justice and redress around money, work and property.

But in an area that matters just as much to us – love and relationships – we can't contact a lawyer or go to the police with an accusation that someone broke our heart. We're on our own. Not only is there no easy way of getting redress, there's little on offer to help us deal with the pain. If we have a toothache or a broken leg (which can be comparable to heartbreak in terms of anguish), we are met by a society that has evolved sophisticated ways of dealing with the problem and built enormous institutions to offer us skilled help.

The point isn't that we should be able to go to a lawyer or a doctor with our complaint; we don't want our ex-partner to be locked up or to undergo some emergency surgery. But we can, in a utopian spirit, imagine a society that has devoted itself with equal ambition – and over many decades – to addressing the intense, common problems of wounded souls.

The broken-heart specialist of the future would carefully listen to our sobs; they might prescribe that we read a particular book or listen to certain pieces of music (like Mozart's opera, *Così fan tutte* – 'Thus Do They All' – in which every lover is shown to let the other down). We could be invited to examine our expectations of relationships and be coaxed gently but firmly towards an understanding of just what went wrong and what we could learn. We might be prompted to reconsider what kinds of people to be wary of, or to seek out, as we re-enter the world of romance.

It has always been hard for us to imagine large societal

responses to private problems – just as in the 17th century it was hard to image the existence of a reliable fire brigade. Relationship endings are standard hazards of existence. And perhaps at some point in the future, people heading off to their broken-heart specialists will look back on us with pity because – when our relationships failed – there were not so many places to turn for wisdom, consolation and guidance.

THE PSYCHOLOGY OF
OUR EXES

In the immediate circumstances of a break-up, we are likely to be focused on what happened in the last few weeks or months to explain the end of a relationship.

But the clue to the failure often has nothing to do with us, and indeed little to do with the actions and feelings of the ex in the present moment. The reason why it all collapsed may lie in their childhood and in the long and typically unexplored path of their psyche towards emotional maturity.

Frustratingly, the way people love as adults sits on top of

experiences of love in their early years – and the capacity to be a reliable and contented partner is in part due to things having gone well with parental figures at the start of their lives.

Unfortunately for relationships, at least half the population is walking around with, and falling in love while beset by, a host of uncharted psychological issues that will make it hugely difficult for them to be predictable and well-attached in relationships. Often, what they ostensibly seek in love is exactly what, in the long run, they cannot accept, for it feels unfamiliar, threatening to their defences and unearned. There is a conflict – of which we end up the unwitting victims – between what they say they seek in a partner, and what they are in fact psychologically capable of accepting.

Perhaps a beloved parent was rather aloof or often

absent in their childhood. When they grew up and began seeking love, the ex may have been drawn to the warmth we offered them, but at the same time, our tenderness would have felt unfamiliar and been perceived as extremely threatening to parts of their personality. They may have struggled to understand what was going on inside themselves when they went cold and had to take their distance from us, but they lacked the tools. It may in the end have felt easier for them to blame us for being 'needy' rather than explore the complicated reasons why their own need was frightening to them. They were replicating a past, doomed and painful version of love, without either of us quite knowing.

Or maybe our ex had a parent who was rather fragile or depressed, or who was impatient or easily irritated. As a result, they learned to be exceedingly cautious around them, always pleasing and putting others' interests first – and never quite letting on what was happening in their hearts, growing isolated and resentful instead. They gravitated towards us, hoping that we would allow them to be themselves. But, while we did our best, dynamics kicked in which meant that they never dared to explain their desires to us properly. They hid what really worried them, they buried away their hurts, they didn't complain as and when they should have done – and eventually, they lost the capacity to feel alive in the relationship.

These thoughts chip away at our worst, most self-punishing interpretations of what happens in our relationships that fail. It is not, as we so quickly fear, that we are invariably revealed as defective; but rather that we have been co-opted into another's fateful private love-dramas, which had their beginnings long before they met us. They didn't manage to love us, but they probably couldn't, at this stage in their emotional evolution, love anyone that well, given the burden bequeathed by their unexplored past.

One of the key questions we should ask a prospective partner on an early date is: 'How did things go in your childhood?' It is often deeply touching to hear that there was pain and loneliness. We may long to fix them and sincerely believe we can, but given the brevity and inherent complexity of existence, we might be better off shedding some of our attractions to movingly damaged people in favour of those who will, boringly but beautifully, love us as we hope and deserve to be loved.

WHY DID WE PICK THEM?

They were perhaps, in the end, not really the right people to pick. As we can see now, they came with a host of problematic points that we would have been wise to steer clear of. But, at the same time, we should graciously accept that we didn't stumble into error by chance. We made a mistake because we often feel actively drawn to the wrong people. The standard view is that we seek happiness in love, but what it seems we actually seek is familiarity – which may well complicate any plans we might have for happiness, for we are not always familiar with what is good for us.

We may unconsciously long to recreate in our adult relationships some of the feelings we knew in childhood. It was as children that we first came to know and understand what love meant. But unfortunately, the lessons we picked up may not have been straightforward. The love we knew then may have come entwined with more than just kindness. It may have been coupled with a feeling of being controlled, or humiliated, being abandoned, never communicating; in short, with suffering.

As adults, we may then reject potential partners, not because they are wrong, but because they are too well-balanced (too mature, too understanding, too reliable), and their rightness feels unfamiliar and somehow oppressive. We may call these kind people 'boring' or 'unsexy' and instead head towards people whom our unconscious senses will frustrate us in familiar ways.

We make mistakes because, deep down, we don't ultimately associate being loved with feeling entirely satisfied.

Knowing that we don't choose our partners freely (from a psychological point of view) can help to dampen our annoyance with those we end up with and who hurt us badly. We weren't merely stupid, we were constrained by our childhood history of love.

Hopefully, the more we understand why certain problematic candidates felt attractive, the more we can free ourselves from their appeal. As we start to grasp how our childhoods gave us unhelpful templates for love, we can free ourselves from their influence and learn to choose partners who can more properly satisfy our adult hopes for happiness and fulfilment.

ATTACHMENT THEORY
– AND BREAK-UPS

There are so many ways to be unhappy in love, but one kind which modern psychology has given particular attention to is relationships in which one of the parties is defined as avoidant in their attachment patterns – and the other as anxious.

Attachment Theory is the term given to a set of ideas about how we love, and the role of childhood therein originally developed by the English psychologist John Bowlby during the fifties and sixties. It divides humanity into three categories according to our varying capacity to behave with confidence and trust in relationships.

Firstly, there are those who are securely attached, who had reliable and good childhood experiences and now expect to be positively treated by those they love. They are fortunate types who are capable of empathy and generosity – and communicate with honesty and directness about their needs. Around fifty percent of the population is assumed to be securely attached.

This leaves two fascinating deviations from health, caused by some form of early parental let-down and trauma. The first kind of attachment pattern is known as 'anxious', the second as 'avoidant'. What makes things even more complicated and very combustible is that anxious and avoidant people are frequently drawn to forming couples (it's part of their pathology) where their varied emotional quirks contribute to an especially fraught combination.

An anxiously attached person in a relationship will have the characteristic feeling of not being properly appreciated and loved. They would – they tell themselves – like so much more closeness, tenderness and physical intimacy, and are convinced that such a union could be possible. The person they are with, however, seems to them humiliatingly and hurtfully detached. They never seem to want them back with as much intensity as they are offered. The anxious lover is hugely saddened by the coldness and distance, and gradually falls into moods of self-loathing and rejection, feeling unappreciated and misunderstood, as well as vengeful and resentful.

For a long time, they might keep quiet about their frustrations until eventually desperation erupts. Even if it is an inappropriate moment (perhaps they and their partner are exhausted and it is past midnight), they won't be able to resist addressing the issues right there and then. Predictably, these sorts of fights go very wrong. The anxious lover loses their calm, they exaggerate and drive their points home with such viciousness that they leave their partner convinced that they are mad and mean.

A securely attached partner might know how to soothe the situation, but an avoidant one certainly doesn't. Tragically, this avoidant party triggers every insecurity known to their anxious lover. Under pressure to be warmer and more connected, the avoidant partner instinctively withdraws and feels overwhelmed and hounded. They go cold and disconnect from the situation, only further ramping up their partner's anxiety. Underneath their silence, the avoidant one resents feeling, as they put it, 'controlled'; they have the impression of being harassed, unfairly persecuted and disturbed by the other's 'neediness'. They may quietly fantasise about going off to have sex with someone else completely, preferably a total stranger, or of going into the other room and reading a book.

It helps immensely to know that this kind of relationship is not unusual; it is a type and there are – quite literally – millions of them unfolding on the planet at any point. Even better, the causes of the distress, which feel so personal and so insulting, are in fact general phenomena, well studied and mapped by sober researchers in lab coats.

The solution, as ever, is simply knowledge. There is an immense difference between acting out on one's anxious or avoidant impulses – and, as would be preferable, understanding that one has them, grasping where they came from and explaining to ourselves and others why they make us do what we do. The majority of us cannot be wholly healthy in love, but we can be something almost as beneficial: We can grow into people committed to explaining our unhealthy, trauma-driven behaviour in good time, before we have become overly furious and hurt others too much – and apologise for our antics after they have run their course. There are few things more romantic, in the true sense, than a couple who have learnt to tell one another with wit and composure that they have been triggered in an anxious or an avoidant direction, but are doing everything they can to get on top of things – and hope to be normal again in a little while.

HOW NOT TO BE TORTURED BY
A LOVE RIVAL

S ometimes, we are not only left in love; we are left for
someone else – a rival who comes to assume a large,
indeed monstrous position in our imaginations. The
torture comes down to one essential question which
pursues us into the early hours:

What do they have that we do not?

Part of the agony rests on a basic feature of human
psychology; we know ourselves from the inside, in great
and dispiriting detail, whereas we can know others
only from the outside, from what they choose to reveal,

which may be almost nothing, aside from an attractive face and a charming manner.

As a result, we may feel that the person we have been left for – whom we know only on the basis of having briefly met at a party or by having stalked their online profile – is accomplished in every way. Where we are shy, they will be confident; where we are chaotic, they will be organised; where our sexuality is complex, theirs will be simple; where we're dull and domestic, they will be exciting ...

Well-meaning friends may try to bring us back into contact with our good sides. They may speak of our kindness, intelligence or sense of fun, but this may not be the best way forward; the point isn't to rehearse how decent we are. To properly get over the pain of a love rival, we need to realise how mediocre pretty much every human who has ever existed tends to be. There is not, in fact, ever any such thing as a 'perfect person'; there are merely differently tricky ones, as our former partner will inevitably learn.

Our failings or defects may well be real but the picture we've got of ourselves as compared with our love rival is skewed by undue ignorance. Recovery does not involve the denial of our less admirable sides: It requires a more nihilistic, and therefore more balanced sense of what people in general are like.

Of course, the rival has qualities we lack. It is true that they have better hair, or a more impressive salary. But at the same time, they have an enormous number of very serious problems, which we can be assured exist, not because we know them, but because we know human beings in general.

No one examined up close is ever anything other than disappointing. Every person we share a life with will prove at points so maddening, we will, on occasion, wish they had never been born. Whatever attractions a new lover can offer our ex, they will also supply them with a whole new set of irritants, which will end up frustrating them as much as we ever did, indeed more so, because they so sincerely hoped – as they packed their bags – that such flaws would not exist in their next partner.

Our ex-lover has not entered the gates of paradise; they have merely exchanged one imperfect relationship for another. We should never compound our grief with the thought that our ex will be uncomplicatedly happy.

The deep lesson of being supplanted is not that we are so bad. It's that we have been left because of a common delusion: the belief that if only we were in a different relationship, we would be substantially happier. Yet the truth is that more or less every relationship has its own special and distinct forms of acute unhappiness.

That there is much wrong with us is, of course, true; but this dark fact invariably sits within a far larger, grimmer and yet strangely consoling truth: that every person has much wrong with them.

Once we get over abandonment, the person we need to find is not the one who thinks we are perfect (and will never leave us on this basis) but rather one who can quite clearly see our failings and yet knows how to calmly make peace with them. The lover we need is not someone who stays with us because they think we are irreplaceable but because they've wisely realised that no one is as attractive as they seem at first – and that to destroy a relationship is generally only a prelude to novel encounters with frustration and disappointment.

HOW TO BREAK UP

The intensity and suffering exacted by a heartbreak depends not only on the core fact that we've been left; it also decisively depends on how we've been left. Our hurt can be hugely intensified when we've been left badly – just as it may be rendered a great deal more bearable when we are fortunate enough to have a lover who has learnt the psychologically rich art of a mature break-up.

There are certain things guaranteed to make a break-up worse than it ever needs to be:

i. *Lingering*

All decisions around relationships should be taken with the awareness that life is desperately short for both parties. It therefore really shouldn't matter that a holiday has already been booked or that preparations for our birthday are – awkwardly – well under way.

As soon as the decision has been taken inwardly, a courageous lover will not dither out of a misplaced desire not to upset pre-existing plans. They know they must leave. They are ruining things, of course, but they can see that the holiday or restaurant meal would in any case be doomed – and they are kind enough to know not to waste any more of anyone's precious time.

ii. *Collateral accusations*

A wise departing lover knows not to accuse the other of more sins than they are guilty of. It is not our fault that their career is going wrong and we truly aren't responsible for their insomnia or conflicts with their brother. The wise lover keeps the list of accusations down to the specific problems that necessitate a break-up; they don't use the parting as an occasion to rehearse all that happens to be a bit wrong with us – an inevitably far longer but irrelevant charge sheet.

iii. Deceptive niceness

The most harmful lovers are those who labour under a misplaced impression that they need to be nice – even when they are breaking up with us. But there is in fact no need for honeyed words; we simply require the basic information and then some privacy to put ourselves back together again. Indeed, ongoing niceness simply confuses us all the more. The tenderness makes us ache to restart the relationship; there seems no reason why not, given how they are behaving. We might even, if we're properly unlucky, end up in bed once more.

iv. Evasiveness

Clumsy lovers are so scared of the news they have to share with us, they cannot bear to come out with it cleanly – and so let it seep out in odd symptomatic ways. They start drinking too much, they come home very late, or advance odd-sounding theories about relationships. They seem to hope – through their perplexing and harmful behaviour – to be pushed rather than to have to jump.

On the other hand, there is so much that can spare us excessive pain:

i. Directness

Kind departing lovers make a sharp break. Once they've decided, they move swiftly to letting us know; they clear off quickly; they don't hold out hints of reconciliation; they don't suggest that if we changed in certain ways, they'd reconsider. It's awful, of course, but there's a vein of mature kindness in their brusque manner: In an obviously difficult situation, they are sparing us the extended torture of false hope.

ii. Clear reasons

Good departing lovers try to explain in convincing ways why the relationship didn't work out. They might point out, for instance, that you are both quite anxious by nature – and therefore struggle to soothe and calm each other. This isn't so much a complaint about you as an observation about why the fit between you as a couple wasn't helpful. Or they may explore the ways in which the two of you have powerfully divergent attitudes to money – and hence are set on a serious collision course. They're not saying you are a fool, just that the two of you turn out not to be very compatible partners for each other.

iii. Honesty about who they are

Compassionate departing lovers let us see and actively remind us of what's not so nice or good about them. They admit that they brought a lot of difficult things into the relationship. Perhaps they're deeply obsessed with their work; they may acknowledge that they are bossy or very controlling; they might be open about their unfaithful nature. They are doing us the kindness of showing us that a life with them would be difficult in major ways. We're losing them, but we're not losing the prospect of a blissful or problem-free future.

iv. Honesty about who we are

Without being aggressive or mean, good departing lovers give us a fair picture of why, in fact, they found it hard to be around us in the end. They're not being bitter or exaggerating: They just fairly and honestly say that, as a matter of fact, they found (for instance) our domestic disorganisation, or our intense neatness, oppressive; they were perhaps unable to come to terms with our very relaxed attitude towards time or our manic punctuality; they found they couldn't live with our sexual complexity or with our austere seriousness. This is hard news, but it's also very constructive and useful. There are few times in life when another person is genuinely frank with us about what we're like to live with. They're not saying that we are bad people: They are showing us that we have a very distinctive personality (which is something it's hard for us to see about ourselves). We're going to have to take this into account in the future if other relationships are to go better. It's not that we have to radically change – and perhaps we can't. But we need, in the future, to factor more of who we are into any relationship with another person. We will have to be frank early on, to ask in good time for forbearance and to realise that we might be daunting or challenging in many areas.

v. Being hated

Good departing lovers know that the news they are breaking will, inevitably, lead to them being hated for a time. They are sanguine and brave in the face of this. They don't suffer from the fateful and sentimental desire to be loved by people they no longer love.

We're gradually disentangling two distinct sources of pain which mean very different things. There's the sorrow of losing someone we liked, but there is also the suffering caused by the unfortunate ways a lover acted at the end which tells us about them, but not really about us. We may not be able to escape the agony of a broken heart but we can always strive to keep the suffering to a wise minimum.

HOW WE CAN BE HEARTBROKEN
EVEN THOUGH THEY HAVEN'T LEFT

It sounds paradoxical: that we can be heartbroken even though a lover is still with us. Yet it's not so strange, because the source of heartbreak is not precisely the physical departure of a lover, but rather the recognition that a partner doesn't really love us any more, something which we may come to realise even without anyone having taken steps to pack their bags.

The physical presence of a lover isn't any sort of guarantee against heartbreak. We might be sharing a bed and bills with a partner – but the love there once was between us may have gone forever. Neither of us is leaving, but we're realising that perhaps for the rest of our lives, we're going to have to exist without the feeling that our partner is delighted by our presence, fascinated by our character and longing to hold and caress us.

We may be very alone with this situation. If someone walks out of the door, there is great cultural support: There are songs and films, condensed bits of wisdom to lean on (plenty more fish in the sea, etc.) and there are some very moving books. People understand and sympathise.

But the death of love in a continuing relationship has been comparatively neglected. There's even a distinct lack of sympathy that surrounds the topic: To a romantically minded culture, it can look rather pitiful to stay together for convenience once passion has gone. If romantic love is everything, then a union without desire is a profoundly offensive proposition.

Yet there might be many good reasons to stay together even when our hearts have, quietly, been broken. It's not what people dream of but our finances are intertwined, there are shared commitments – perhaps even children – we've developed friends in common, we've established ways of living together that might be both convenient to us and a great help to others – and there won't be too many people available who are keen to start a new relationship with someone like us. So we may be wise to stick where we are, despite the deep vein of sorrow and sense of loss that accompanies us through the long evenings.

The support we need is the realisation that, though the situation is painful and undiscussed, it is not for that matter strange or shameful. It is extremely ordinary and even rather noble. If we left and found someone else, we'd probably end up in the same position a few years later – because, in some ways, love almost always dies. The romantic intensity that marked those early years isn't a description of life together in the long term.

There are, of course, a few exceptions – but we make the mistake of supposing that because very occasionally a couple stays in love for many years, this is a common occurrence. Instead, we should see it the way we might view certain jobs. Of course it's possible for someone to make a great living by being a stand-up comic, but this is realistically only an option for a very few, deeply unusual individuals: It tells us nothing about what is possible for us.

If we are in a relationship where love has died, we are not particularly missing out, we have not particularly failed: We are simply meeting an ordinary, yet rarely described, fate.

THE WIDER CONTEXT
OF OUR SORROW

When a lover leaves us, we are acutely aware of the uniqueness of our pain. But, in the interests of soothing our agonies, it may serve us well to remember the connection between heartbreak and other forms of dereliction.

In one way or another, loss is everywhere; it is the ubiquitous experience of all members of our species – and to keep this in mind is to connect our lonely sorrow with the griefs of humanity more broadly. Hearts are continuously being broken in so many ways by reality.

The world is made of heartbreak, so when we meet rejection in love we're plunged not only into our own private sorrow, but into the fundamental agony of the human condition. We are miserable, but we are also strangely glorious: because we are, at least for a while, alert to the essential woe of life. We are entering – ideally – into communion with the widest and deepest examples of loss.

At its best, our suffering renders us more compassionate because it draws us closer to the hidden truth of all people: To live is to suffer. Our pain stops being purely personal and becomes a tender lament for the imprecisely known, but utterly real, sorrows of strangers.

Hearts are continuously being broken...
The fact that everyone who once lived in this photo is now dead.

WHY WE REQUIRE POOR
MEMORIES TO SURVIVE

Generally our culture takes a very positive view of memories and the act of remembering: We esteem the study of history, we are expected to take photos to capture precious moments, we think that old injustices should be made good in the present, we promise not to forget old acquaintances and we try hard in psychotherapy to reassemble the emotional essence of our childhoods.

But without denying the value of any of this, it pays to honour the idea that in order to survive, we actively also need to do something else: forget. Certain memories threaten to destroy the future – and our capacity to exist. If we held onto everything that had ever happened to us in all the technicolour vividness of the original event, we'd be overburdened with anxiety and sadness; we'd be continuously terrified and consumed with regret; we'd be driven to despair by all the meanness we'd encountered, all the stupidity we'd been guilty of and all the beauty and goodness we had lost. To have a poor memory contributes, in many contexts, to survival.

In the 1870s, the German philosopher Friedrich Nietzsche circled this theme in an essay called 'On the Use and Abuse of History for Life'. Though Nietzsche was himself a brilliant historian and hugely aware of political and social history, he also came to recognise that forgetting was essential to a capacity to thrive, at both an individual and collective level. As he put it:

There is a degree of insomnia, of rumination, of the historical sense, through which living comes to harm and finally is destroyed, whether it is a person or a people or a culture.

Nietzsche attributed the vigour and natural stoicism of animals to their ignorance of the past. If a cow knew all that had happened to her forebears, her life would feel impossible, the philosopher speculated. Analogously, he proposed that children can be moving to us precisely because they aren't burdened by the memories and regrets that start to dampen the spirits of anyone past twenty-five; nothing much has yet happened to the very young, and therefore so much more seems possible.

Nietzsche was approaching a radical but properly constructive question: What is the point of thinking about the past? His answer was precise: We should remember only in so far as it actually helps us to live in the present. To the extent that memories assist us in forming our plans and avoiding error, they are valuable, but when memories function as obstacles to better lives, we should put our energies into the business of forgetting.

The best way to forget is not just time, but – more exactly – events. So as to separate ourselves from the things that haunt us, we have to ensure that we can lay down a dense layer of events between ourselves and them; we need – in short – to make stuff happen.

This is particularly true after a bad break-up, when certain places, times of day and activities remain imaginatively linked to the past and constantly evoke it painfully:

- When we see the pizza restaurant at the end of the road, we agonisingly recall cosy Sunday evenings there together.
- Riding a bike down the canal triggers thoughts of impromptu trips we made there on balmy days.
- The cushions on the sofa painfully jab us, reminding us of the way our lover would use them while reading at night.

We're surrounded by emotional tripwires. Our heart breaks again and again.

We cannot, as we might at points want to, get rid of the world in which the relationship once played itself out. We can't burn the cushions or uproot the restaurant. To forget, we have to impose a new layer of experience on the things we associate with lost love. We should take a new group of friends to the pizza place, sit at the side of the canal with a kind of book that particularly impresses us or get fresh acquaintances to hang out with us on the sofa. We have to reclaim the material of our lives from the person who broke our heart.

With a new commitment to forgetting, we can recover some of the hope of the child and the fortitude of a cow.

OUR LOVER WAS
NOT UNIQUE

They've gone and we miss them so much. No one can replace them: It feels as if we'll never be happy again. A well-intentioned friend might advise us to just not think about them. But curiously it may be wiser, and ultimately more helpful, to force ourselves – if we can – to go over in our minds exactly what it is we miss about them.

Instead of just saying that we miss them, we can try to define what, precisely, piece by piece, was so nice about the relationship. Maybe they had a particularly sweet smile, or perhaps we were attracted to their worldly sophistication; it was great at the end of a difficult day to joke with them about our annoying colleagues; or maybe they gave us confidence at parties; perhaps we like that they introduced us to their genial friends or understood us so well in bed ...

When we say we miss them what we really mean is that it is a set of good qualities and experiences that we are missing. It is tenderness, conviviality and open-mindedness we love, first and foremost rather than, inherently, the bodily home in which these qualities came to rest. We encountered these things in and with them and so assume that to lose the person is to lose everything linked to them.

We're right to miss the good things: We still need to see a sweet smile, we still need to encounter sophistication;

we need cosiness and confidence and to be understood sexually. It's true that we'll never meet another person exactly like the lover we have just lost. They were unique. But the good things we met in and through them are general: They are available elsewhere – not all bundled up into one person in exactly this way but distributed more widely across the species.

Other versions of such smiles exist, other versions of their sophisticated, slightly cynical take on life, other capacities to make ambitious weekend plans or laugh at pomposity. In losing one person, we can't logically forever have lost contact with the elements that made them valuable – and that continue to exist, scattered throughout humanity.

One of the odder – and more profound – lessons of a broken heart is the eventual realisation that the focus of our love is not really an individual person but a range of good things which – thankfully – cannot be the unique property of a single person but can be found in other potential partners, waiting for us to be ready to encounter them as soon as we are stronger.

THE CONSOLATIONS
OF FRIENDSHIP

One of the most subtly hurtful and quietly damning of all remarks, perhaps quietly and sweetly delivered on the doorstep at the end of a long evening, with a taxi hovering somewhere just out of sight, is the suggestion that we should in the end probably remain 'just good friends'.

We know exactly what to understand by this. The path towards a tender future is being gently but firmly closed off. We are, with a smile, being shunted into the category of the failed and the scorned. They must have worked out the embarrassing truths about us – all the ones that we tried so hard to disguise and even to believe didn't exist – and have logically decided to take their leave. We return home crushed to an empty room that we left with butterflies and elevated hopes only a few hours before.

We hear the invitation of friendship as synonymous with insult because our romantic culture has continuously, and from a young age, made one thing sharply clear to us: Love is the purpose of existence; friendship is the paltry, depleted consolation prize.

Though this may seem like common sense, what should detain us and encourage us to probe a little at the claims made on love's behalf is one basic source of evidence: the behaviour, level of satisfaction and state of mind of those who engage in it.

If we were to judge love chiefly by its negative impact – the extent of the tears, the depths of the frustrations, the viciousness of the insults that unfold in its name – we would not continue to revere it as we do and might indeed mistake it for a form of illness or aberration of the mind. The scenes that typically unfold between sniping lovers would scarcely be considered imaginable outside of conditions of open hostility.

Those we love, we honour with our worst moods, our most unfair accusations, our most wounding insults. It is to our lovers that we direct blame for everything that has gone wrong in our lives, it is they we expect to know everything we mean without bothering to explain it, it is to their minor errors and misunderstandings that we respond with sulks and rage.

By comparison, in friendship – the supposedly worthless

and inferior state whose mention should crush us at the end of a date – we bring our highest and noblest virtues. Here we are patient, encouraging, tolerant, funny and – most of all – kind. We expect a little less and therefore, by extension, forgive an infinite amount more. We do not presume that we will be fully understood by one single individual, and so treat failings lightly and humanely. We don't imagine that our friends should admire us without reserve and stick by us whatever we do, and so we put in effort and behave, pleasing ourselves as well as our companions along the way. We are, in the company of our friends, our best selves.

Paradoxically, it is friendship that often offers us the real route to the pleasures that Romanticism associates with love. That this sounds surprising is only a reflection of how underdeveloped our day-to-day vision of friendship has become. We associate it with a casual acquaintance we see only occasionally to exchange inconsequential banter. But real friendship is something altogether more profound: It is an arena in which two people can get a sense of each other's vulnerabilities, appreciate each other's follies without recrimination, reassure one another as to their value and greet the sorrows and tragedies of existence with wit and warmth.

Culturally and collectively, we have made a momentous mistake which has left us both lonelier and more disappointed than we ever needed to be. In a better world, our most serious goal would not be to locate one special lover with whom to replace all other humans, it would be to put our intelligence and energy into identifying and nurturing a circle of true friends. At the end of an evening, we would learn to say to certain prospective companions, with an embarrassed smile as we invited them inside – knowing that this would come across as a painful rejection – 'I'm so sorry, couldn't we just be … lovers?'

THE BENEFITS OF
A BROKEN HEART

It is not at all what we would have chosen for ourselves, or wished on anyone else, but there are – amidst the ruins – some benefits to be discovered (and quietly celebrated) around the business of having our hearts broken:

i. It hurt horribly, we were convinced we would die from the pain, and yet, remarkably we have not. We are still around and will, next week, go to a party. We reach a rather extraordinary conclusion: We have managed to survive. And so, we can conclude: We are a great deal stronger than we originally anticipated.

ii. We have understood so much more about ourselves. The lessons were delivered in a grim way, of course, but through all the recriminations and accusations, the arguments and the tensions, we learnt things. We have come to recognise – in calmer moments – that we are really rather difficult to live with, a crucial realisation upon which our capacity to be a little easier to be with in the future can develop.

iii. As we recover, we realise that our inner contentment isn't entirely dependent on any one person in particular. There are many people and things that can sustain and support us. The great love has gone, but many other loves are still open to us. We become more appreciative of what remains to us: There are many captivating books to read, new foods to try, the park is coated with enchanting flowers, we have friends who will put up with our calls late into the night. There is so much left to love.

iv. We learn to temper our expectations. All relationships are seriously imperfect in certain respects; we should endeavour to not ask quite so much of the next person we are with. We will know to be grateful for 'good enough'.

v. We have gone through one of the universal sorrows of humanity. We rarely hear about the broken hearts of others, but we know that almost everyone has their own version of our sorrow (or will have one day). Our compassion for our fellow humans, and hence also for ourselves, becomes deeper and wider. We grow kinder and, in some moods, a little readier to laugh warmly at the absurdities and contradictions of the heart.

THE LOVE SERIES

There is no more joyful or troublesome area of our lives than love. From adolescence onwards, it is rare to go for any sustained length of time without some sort of fascinating or devilish new problem emerging around relationships.

The Love Series by The School of Life aims to be like an ideal friend around the dilemmas of the heart. Each title zeroes in on one of the central issues we're liable to confront – from dating to heartbreak, from affairs to arguments. What unites the books is their combination of psychological insight, humanity and warmth: They lend us the advice and comfort we need to find the happiness we deserve.